My business is to succeed,
and I'm good at it.

Napoleon to Pope Pius VII in 1804

For Leo

Who would have seen Napoleon steadily and seen him whole

Photographs © 2010: akg-Images, London: 80 top (Catherine Bibollet), 66 (Jérôme da Cunha), 77 center, 78 bottom (Laurent Lecat), 105 (VISIOARS), 14, 19, 23, 29, 39, 53, 54, 57, 69, 76 top, 77 top, 78 top, 79 bottom, 81 top, 86, 89, 92, 112; Art Resource, NY: 110 (Bildarchiv Preussischer Kulturbesitz), 73 (Bridgeman-Giraudon), 79 top (Erich Lessing), 81 center (Musée de l'Armee), 48, 63, 77 bottom, 81 bottom, 118, 119 (Réunion des Musées Nationaux), 41 (Scala); Bridgeman Art Library International Ltd., London/New York: 103 (Bibliotheque Nationale, Paris), 95 (Chateau de Versailles, France), 116 (National Army Museum, London), 100 (Prado, Madrid), 10 (Private Collection/©Agnew's, London); Mary Evans Picture Library: 58; The Granger Collection, New York: 34, 76 bottom, 80 bottom (Rue des Archives), 27, 76 center, 80 center.

Illustrations by XNR Productions, Inc.: 4, 5, 8, 9
Cover art, page 8 inset by Mark Summers
Chapter art by Raphael Montoliu

Library of Congress Cataloging-in-Publication Data
· Heuston, Kimberley Burton, 1960–
Napoleon: emperor and conqueror / Kimberley Heuston.
p. cm. — (A wicked history)
Includes bibliographical references and index.
ISBN-13: 978-0-531-21277-6 (lib. bdg.) 978-0-531-22823-4 (pbk.)
ISBN-10: 0-531-21277-7 (lib. bdg.) 0-531-22823-1 (pbk.)
1. Napoleon I, Emperor of the French, 1769–1821—Juvenile literature.
2. France—History—1789–1815—Juvenile literature. 3.
Emperors—France—Biography—Juvenile literature. I. Title.
DC203.H57 2009
944.05'092—dc22
[B]

2009016539

Tod Olson, Series Editor
Marie O'Neill, Art Director
Allicette Torres, Cover Design
SimonSays Design!, Book Design and Production

© 2010 Scholastic Inc.

11 12 13 14 15 R 19 18 17 16 15 14 13

A WiCKED HISTORY™

Napoleon

Emperor and Conqueror

KIMBERLEY HEUSTON

Franklin Watts®
An Imprint of Scholastic Inc.
New York Toronto London Auckland Sydney
Mexico City New Delhi Hong Kong
Danbury, Connecticut

The World of Napoleon Bonaparte

As emperor of France, Napoleon plunged Europe into a
constant state of war that lasted more than a decade.

Borodino• ☿ Moscow
Ⓕ

N

RUSSIA

KEY

Ⓐ Napoleon was born in 1769.

Ⓑ In 1793, Napoleon won his first battle by driving French Royalists from Toulon.

Ⓒ Returning from Egypt in 1799 as a military hero, Napoleon seized control of the French government.

Ⓓ A British fleet crushed the combined French-Spanish navy in 1805, dooming Napoleon's plan to invade Britain.

Ⓔ Just six weeks after Trafalgar, Napoleon defeated a combined Austro-Russian army in the greatest victory of his career.

Ⓕ Napoleon's 600,000-man army was devastated during a disastrous retreat from Moscow in 1812.

Ⓖ In 1813, the combined armies of Austria, Russia, Prussia, and Sweden outlasted Napoleon at the brutal Battle of Nations.

Ⓗ Napoleon suffered his final defeat in 1815 and was exiled.

French Empire in 1810
States ruled by Napoleon's family
Other dependent states

Danube R.

Black Sea

OTTOMAN EMPIRE

SYRIA

miles
0   200   400

0   200   400
kilometers

Alexandria
EGYPT   •Cairo

TABLE OF CONTENTS

A Wicked Web

A look at the allies and enemies of Napoleon Bonaparte.

Family and Allies

∽∾∽∾∽∾∽∾∽∾∽∾∽∾∽∾∽∾∽∾

LETIZIA BUONAPARTE — CARLO BUONAPARTE
his mother · his father

JOSEPH, LUCIEN, LOUIS,
AND JEROME
his brothers

ELISA, PAULINE,
AND CAROLINE
his sisters

JOSEPHINE
his first wife

HORTENSE AND EUGENE
his stepchildren

NAPOLEON
BONAPARTE

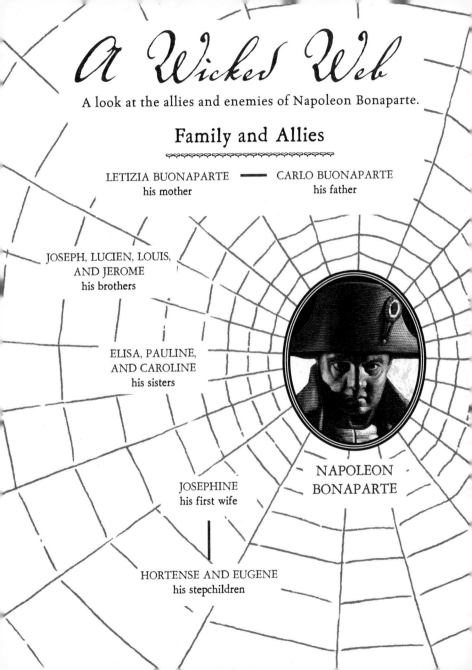

MARIE-LOUISE
his second wife

NAPOLEON II
their son

JOSEPH FOUCHÉ
his chief of police

Enemies and Opponents

HORATIO NELSON
commander of the
British navy

DUKE OF WELLINGTON
commander of the
British army

ALEXANDER I
tsar of Russia

FRANCIS I
emperor of Austria

LOUIS XVIII
king of France during
Napoleon's exile on Elba

NAPOLEON BONAPARTE, 1769–1821

THE ARMIES HAD BEEN FIGHTING FOR hours in the pre-dawn darkness, wrapped in a cold mist that deadened every sense—except fear. Slowly, the fog became visible and then thinned in the sun, revealing a staggering sight: 150,000 men fighting for their lives amid screaming horses and splintered trees. Severed body parts, still warm enough to steam gently in the frosty air, littered the battlefield.

On a rise overlooking the field, Europe's two most powerful monarchs sat side by side on their splendid horses. Francis I of Austria watched as his men fought for the rich soil his family had ruled for centuries. His tall, stiff posture and heavily decorated uniform suited an emperor who ruled all of Central Europe.

His ally, Tsar Alexander I of Russia, cut an equally impressive figure. He was blond and handsome. Though only 27 years old, he snapped out orders so confidently that no one would have guessed that this was his first major battle.

Francis and Alexander had reason to be confident. They had more men and twice as many heavy guns as their French opponents. Their troops controlled the high ground at the center of the battlefield.

The French, on the other hand, were far from home and surrounded by hostile nations. Their army may once have been strong, but repeated battles had worn it down. Scouts reported signs that their south flank was particularly weak.

The Austrian and Russian generals listened to the reports and advised an all-out assault on the southern side of the French line. The rulers agreed.

Several miles away, a pale man with stringy dark hair paced his exhausted horse back and forth. The French commander seemed to have nothing in common with his rivals on the other side of the battlefield. He wore no splendid uniform—just an ordinary gray cloth coat. He was not descended from one of the great families of Europe. And yet exactly one year ago, Napoleon Bonaparte had brazenly crowned himself as France's first emperor in 900 years.

Napoleon brought his horse to an abrupt stop. Through the rising mist, he saw enemy soldiers on the move, deserting the center of their line to attack his south flank. *Stupid fools*, Napoleon thought with contempt. *Never, never weaken your center.*

Napoleon put up a hand, summoning one of his generals to his side. "One sharp blow and the war is over," he said.

As the sun broke through the fog, wave after wave of French troops battered the weak center their commander had spotted. Within a few hours, it was all over. The French had broken through the enemy line and surrounded the Austrian and Russian armies. Francis and Alexander had no choice but to surrender.

That night, Emperor Francis I sat in his tent, a shattered man. Two of every five men he'd commanded that morning had been killed, wounded, or taken

NAPOLEON (on white horse) celebrates his victory at the Battle of Austerlitz. The brilliant French general weakened his south flank to lure the Austrians and Russians into attacking. Then he demolished his opponents with a vicious counterstrike.

captive. He had lost the war—and with it his claim to lands from Italy in the south to the Netherlands in the north.

The emperor's young ally, Alexander, was nowhere to be found. Eventually, some officers would come upon the tsar miles from the battlefield, sitting alone under a tree, sobbing bitterly into his handkerchief.

As darkness fell, Emperor Napoleon was still walking the battlefield. It was a dreadful scene, strewn with 15,000 corpses. But he couldn't keep a smile from tugging at his lips. He had done it. He had won control of Italy, Belgium, the Netherlands, and much of Germany. And he had showed everyone that real power didn't come from family and privilege, but from talent and determination.

And it was only the beginning. Give him ten years—15 at the most—and he would shape Europe into the strongest, fairest, most efficient and prosperous state the world had ever known.

"This is," Bonaparte told an aide, gesturing at the bodies heaped around him, "the happiest day of my life."

PART 1

A Taste for Power

CHAPTER 1

Born to Fight

With revolutionaries for parents,
young Buonaparte decides he
WANTS TO BE A SOLDIER.

ON AUGUST 15, 1769, A PREGNANT TEENAGER
named Letizia Buonaparte went to Mass at the
cathedral near her home in the Corsican capital
of Ajaccio. Partway through the service, she went
into labor. She made it home just in time to deliver
a scrawny child with an unusually oversized head.
Letizia and her husband, Carlo, gave the boy an
odd name, Nabullione, after a relative who had
recently died.

It was an unlikely beginning for France's future emperor. For one thing, Nabullione's parents hated everything French. Corsica, a rugged island off the coast of Italy, had just been sold to France by its Italian rulers. French troops swarmed the island, enraging the Corsican people. Just before their son's birth, the Buonapartes had joined a rebellion against French rule. They spent the first half of Letizia's pregnancy hiding from the French in a series of caves.

NABULLIONE BUONAPARTE was born in Corsica, an island nation that had recently come under France's control.

Although the rebellion was crushed a few months before Nabullione's birth, Letizia loved to tell stories about those exciting times. As a child, little Nabullione was happy to listen. He could easily imagine his brave, decisive mother as a rebel fighter.

Privately, he doubted that his father had really been as daring. Carlo had given up fighting the French rulers of Corsica and taken a job with them instead. To his son, he seemed lazy and indecisive. He was also careless with money—"too fond of pleasure," Nabullione decided.

Nabullione and his older brother, Joseph, were soon joined by five new siblings, but Nabullione didn't feel close to any of them. He was a difficult, unattractive child. He lied to get his way, even though he was beaten for it. When things didn't go the way he wished, he sulked and threw tantrums. He even disliked his name, which he found "virile and poetic— altogether excessive." He demanded that his family call him "Buonaparte."

"I was a mean one, always spoiling for a fight," he later admitted. "I would pound on one boy, and scratch another. They were all afraid of me."

Early in his life, Buonaparte decided that he wanted to be a soldier. He drew battle formations all over the family playroom. He befriended the French soldiers guarding Ajaccio and talked them into trading their coarse army rations for his lunch. His favorite toy was a small brass cannon that could be packed with real gunpowder and then set off, shaking the entire house and making his little sisters scream.

When Buonaparte was nine years old, his father used his government contacts to get his son a scholarship at a military school in France. Buonaparte was furious. Why would his parents send him to live with their hated French enemies? Because, his father told him coldly, it was the French who had won. If Buonaparte wanted to succeed in life, he must learn their ways.

And so, late in 1778, young Buonaparte left the island he loved to become a French soldier.

C H A P T E R 2

Going French

Buonaparte learns about
the world FROM HIS COUNTRY'S
SWORN ENEMY.

BUONAPARTE HATED FRANCE JUST AS
much as he thought he would. French society was
rigidly divided according to social rank. Those who
were born into noble families had all the privileges
and looked down on everyone else.

Buonaparte's French classmates, all of them members
of the nobility, refused to accept a newcomer from
Corsica as one of their own. When Buonaparte lost his
temper, they called him a "Corsican savage" and said

BUONAPARTE takes part in a snowball fight with his classmates.
Buonaparte enjoyed his schoolwork, but he hated France.

he belonged in a zoo with the rest of his countrymen. When he tried to blend in, they made fun of his shabby clothes and his clumsy French.

Trying to ignore the abuse, Buonaparte devoted himself to his studies. He improved his French and found he had a gift for math. He also displayed a talent for military strategy, organizing winter war games among his classmates. For ammunition he used "ice bullets" made by packing pebbles in wet snow.

After six years, Buonaparte had done well enough to be admitted to one of Europe's most prestigious military academies: the École Militaire. At the age of 15, he traveled to the dazzling city of Paris and moved into comfortable quarters at the school. Each cadet had a private room and a servant. Most of the students came from wealthy backgrounds and felt right at home.

Buonaparte, however, was disgusted by the École Militaire. Future officers needed discipline not pampering, he complained. Even worse, graduates from the most important families tended to get the best posts, regardless of their abilities.

The young Corsican was not optimistic about his future in the French army, but he kept working hard. While his classmates spent their free hours drinking, gambling, and romancing pretty girls, Buonaparte stayed in his room studying military history and philosophy.

Four months after his arrival at the École Militaire, Buonaparte received devastating news: His father had died of stomach cancer. The family had lost its main source of income, so Letizia had decided to withdraw her other children from school. But Buonaparte, she insisted, should stay where he was. The family needed at least one successful member to support them in the future.

Devoted as he was to his mother, Buonaparte felt a heavy weight on his shoulders. "Even when I had finished my work and had nothing to do," he later remembered, "I vaguely felt that time was fleeting and I had not a moment to lose."

Wasting no time at all, Buonaparte raced through the École Militaire in a year instead of the usual two or three. In October 1785, at the age of 16, he received his commission as a second lieutenant, becoming one of the youngest officers in the history of the French military.

Buonaparte was pleased to win a post with an artillery regiment in the south of France. At the time, aiming and firing large guns was a complicated affair that involved a lot of mathematical calculations.

Artillery was one of the few branches of the military where promotions depended on talent instead of social rank.

As an eager young officer, Buonaparte impressed his superiors with detailed research on topics such as the positioning of guns during battle. But his obligations to his family kept interrupting his military career. Over the next three years, he spent half his time on leave in Corsica, helping his mother set up a business that would support the family.

While Buonaparte was away in Corsica, a revolution was brewing in France. It would shock the world, plunge the country into a bloody civil war, and change the young soldier's life forever.

ROOTS OF REVOLT

FOR CENTURIES, FRANCE HAD BEEN RULED by aristocrats whose word was law. A small group of wealthy nobles owned most of the land and didn't have to pay taxes. Only nobles had the right to be officers in the army or act as judge and jury in their communities.

For several decades, French philosophers had tried to persuade their countrymen that it was time for a change. They argued that all people—not just the wealthy—had a right to think and act for themselves. Everyone, they insisted, should be equal under the law.

By the summer of 1789, their ideas had caught on. Several bad harvests in a row had left peasants starving and laborers out of work.

Revolution was in the air.

WOMEN IN PARIS
riot for bread in 1789.

CHAPTER 3

Revolution!

CHAOS IN FRANCE gives Buonaparte new opportunities.

IN JULY 1789, BUONAPARTE WAS ENJOYING artillery school in eastern France when the country erupted in revolt. A hundred miles away in Paris, a rebellious mob stormed the Bastille, a notorious jail that held political enemies of the government. As fighting raged in the streets, representatives in France's legislature, the National Assembly, seized control of the government. They passed the Declaration of the Rights of Man, which proclaimed that everyone—even their king, Louis XVI—was

THE FRENCH REVOLUTION began when an angry mob stormed the Bastille, a fortress and prison in central Paris. To the rioters, the Bastille was a powerful symbol of the monarchy's evils.

to have the same rights and responsibilities under the law.

The French Revolution had begun, with its leaders fighting to overturn the monarchy under the rallying cry, "liberty, equality, fraternity." The promise of equality filled Buonaparte with hope. He had a much better chance to succeed in a society that rewarded men for their abilities, not just their families' social status. "Revolutions are ideal times for soldiers with a bit of wit and the courage to act," he wrote to a friend.

In September 1789, Buonaparte returned to Corsica, brimming with enthusiasm for the revolution. He organized a "revolutionary club" and tried to form a volunteer militia to fight for revolutionary goals. He also helped convince the National Assembly in Paris to give the Corsican people all the rights of French citizens.

The Corsicans, however, weren't sure they wanted Buonaparte's help. The French governor of the island supported the king, not the revolutionaries. And many Corsicans wanted independence from France, not French citizenship. Buonaparte's efforts on behalf of the revolution got him temporarily expelled from the Corsican capital near the end of the year.

Returning to France, he found the revolution getting more and more radical by the day. In 1790, the government seized all the property of the Catholic

Church in France. The following June, King Louis XVI and Queen Marie Antoinette tried to flee the country. They were arrested and placed under guard. Before long they were executed, their heads severed from their bodies by a killing machine known as the guillotine.

France became a republic—a nation ruled by elected representatives instead of a king.

Then the new nation descended into civil war. Thousands of nobles who had lost their privileges fled to neighboring countries and began plotting to overthrow the republic. Those who remained in France joined with Catholic peasants and took up arms against the new government. The rebels were known as "Royalists" for their support of the monarchy. In Paris, the leaders of the republic sent suspected Royalists to the guillotine by the thousands.

Soon the conflict spread to the rest of Europe. In the spring of 1792, French Republicans declared war against Austria, claiming that Royalist refugees there were planning to attack.

The rulers of other European countries sided with Austria. After all, the French Republicans had not only overthrown their king, they were urging people in other countries to do the same. In 1793, the kings of Great Britain, Prussia, Spain, Portugal, Austria, and several Italian nations formed a coalition to restore the monarchy to France—and silence the Republicans.

While war raged on the borders of France, Buonaparte was back in Corsica trying to win support for the republic. But the Corsicans, more than anything, wanted to be done with France. They had gotten rid of their Royalist governor and had elected leaders who supported full independence for the island. Buonaparte was denounced as a traitor for his allegiance to the French Republic. A mob marched to his family home and ransacked it while Letizia and her children hid outside in the shrubbery.

In June, the family gathered on the coast of Corsica, boarded a boat, and fled for their lives to France. They had little more than the clothes on their backs.

CHAPTER 4

In Command

Buonaparte finds his place—
IN THE TRENCHES.

THE BUONAPARTES ARRIVED IN THE south of France with no money, no home, and only Nabullione's army pay to support them.

Nabullione Buonaparte was 23 years old. His family had been torn from the island they loved. War was breaking their new country apart. Supporting a large family in such conditions was a heavy burden.

But since his early days in Corsica, Buonaparte had dreamed of becoming a soldier. Now, there was a real war to fight, and he was determined to make a name for

IN 1793, BUONAPARTE got his first taste of glory when his outnumbered troops seized Toulon, a Royalist stronghold in southern France.

himself. He asked his superiors for a new post. They were desperate for officers because so many nobles had fled the French army. Buonaparte was made a captain in one of the artillery companies on France's southern coast.

Buonaparte got his family settled in the city of Marseilles and then left for his new command. Before he arrived, a crisis in the city of Toulon gave him just the opportunity he so desperately wanted.

With help from the British navy, Royalists had seized control of Toulon. A Republican army sent from Paris surrounded the city, but its artillery commander had been badly wounded. Thanks to a Corsican friend who held a high position in the Republican government, Buonaparte was given the command.

Buonaparte left at once for Toulon, where he took over the artillery batteries besieging the city. As he surveyed his arsenal, the enormity of the task sunk in. The Republican army had only a handful of cannons, while the Royalists had more than a hundred. An envoy from the National Assembly in Paris had recently judged the situation hopeless and recommended giving up the entire region to the Royalists.

Buonaparte would have none of it. He made a plan and sent it to the Ministry of War in Paris with a promise that he would retake Toulon. Then he organized his troops into squads and led them on scavenging missions through the countryside. They returned with cannons, wagons, horses, heavy beams, even new recruits.

On December 14, 1793, Buonaparte aimed his new guns at a hilltop fortress occupied by the Royalists and opened fire. His men stormed the fort and turned their cannons on the British ships in the harbor below. As he later recalled, "Artillery diligently fed by red-hot cannonballs is terrible against a fleet."

Within hours, the Royalists surrendered and the British fleet sailed for home.

To make sure his superiors knew whom to thank for the victory, Buonaparte fired off a report to the Ministry of War. "I promised you brilliant successes," he wrote, "and, as you see, I have kept my word."

For his brilliance at Toulon, Buonaparte was quickly promoted to brigadier general. To show their commitment to their new country, he and his family changed the spelling of their name to Bonaparte— the French spelling of their Italian name. They had come a long way from the dark times of the previous summer—and Toulon was only the beginning.

C H A P T E R   5

Success in Paris

Bonaparte spreads terror
as he gives the Royalists a
"WHIFF OF GRAPESHOT."

A FTER TOULON, BONAPARTE'S REPUTATION
as a brilliant strategist spread quickly. "Words fail
me to describe Bonaparte's merits," his commanding
officer wrote to the minister of war. "He has plenty
of knowledge, and as much intelligence and courage.
And that is no more than a first sketch of the virtues
of a most rare officer."

Still, despite his growing reputation, Bonaparte was
unable to secure a position he felt was worthy of his

37

talents. In May 1795, he moved to Paris, hoping to badger the Republican leaders into giving him a better command. But the wars against the coalition nations were going badly, and the republic was losing the support of the French people. The government was too busy trying to save itself to worry about a young soldier with muddy boots and clumsy manners—no matter what he had done at Toulon.

On October 3, Royalists rose up against the government, sending 30,000 protesters into the streets of Paris. Bonaparte made his way to government offices in the Tuileries Palace, where the country's panicked leaders gave him command of 5,000 soldiers.

Bonaparte quickly sent an aide to gather guns and men while he scouted the area and planned a defense. When the Royalists struck, he was ready. As the most influential men in Paris cowered in the Tuileries, he turned his guns on an advancing crowd. When the barrage ended, 1,400 protesters lay dead in the streets.

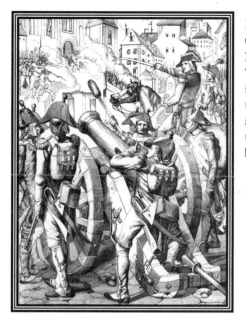

BONAPARTE FIRES GRAPESHOT into a Royalist mob in Paris. "They put the matter in my hands," Bonaparte told critics of the massacre. "It is only fair that I should do the business my own way."

Bonaparte quickly became the toast of Paris, a dashing hero who had saved the republic. "Muddy boots were now out of the question," a friend of his mother's remembered. "[He] had become a necessary and important personage, and all as if by magic."

The grateful leaders of the republic promoted Bonaparte to full general. With his new salary, the family finances were no longer a problem. Bonaparte moved his mother and sisters to a beautiful apartment in the center of Paris. He sent his youngest brother to a good school and arranged well-paid government positions for his other brothers.

Amid the whirl of parties and dinners that followed his promotion, Bonaparte was often thrown together with a widow named Rose de Beauharnais. Unlike Bonaparte, who could never completely shake his Corsican roots, Rose felt perfectly at home in the drawing rooms of Paris. He was awed by her warmth and charm and fell madly in love. To everyone's surprise, he even had a soft spot for her two young children, Hortense and Eugene.

Bonaparte was a demanding suitor. He didn't care for the name Rose and insisted that she change her name to Josephine. But he genuinely adored her and deluged her with passionate love letters. "I awake every day with thoughts only of you. . . . Sweet and incomparable Josephine, what a strange effect you have on me!"

Josephine did not show the same enthusiasm for Bonaparte. But she was 33. At the time, that was old

IN 1795, BONAPARTE FELL IN LOVE with Josephine de Beauharnais. Time spent without her, he wrote, was "hopeless sorrow, inconsolable misery, sadness without end."

for an unmarried woman with two children. She worried that if she didn't accept him, she might not get another offer.

So, on the evening of March 9, 1796, Josephine and Bonaparte were married. Bonaparte had just been named commander of the French army in Italy. Two days later, he left Paris and his new bride to take up his new command.

PART 2

General
Bonaparte

CHAPTER 6

The War in Italy

The Little Corporal
defeats continental Europe's
GREATEST EMPIRE.

BY THE TIME BONAPARTE LEFT FOR ITALY, the Republican army had quieted most of the Royalists within the borders of France. French troops had also seized Belgium and the Netherlands from Austria.

But the members of the coalition—Austria, Great Britain, and several Italian states—were still determined to destroy the French Republic. Austrian troops occupied a 600-mile line along France's eastern border, from Belgium in the north to Italy in the south.

Since 1792, the French had fought a seesaw war along the border, seizing territory and then losing it again. Now, Bonaparte and his fellow generals decided it was time for a decisive attack. Two armies would cross the Rhine River in the north and center of France, and then press toward the Austrian capital of Vienna. Bonaparte would lead a third attack from Italy, in the south.

Late in March 1796, Bonaparte arrived in Nice, on the Italian border, to take command of his army. He got a surly welcome from his new troops. They were on the verge of mutiny after months of inadequate food, shelter, clothing, ammunition, and pay. And at first glance, their new general did not inspire confidence. He was inexperienced, lacked the manners of a gentleman, and spoke French with a heavy Corsican accent.

Bonaparte's actions quickly made up for his appearance. Appalled by the conditions faced by his soldiers, he pressed supply officers for boots, guns, and blankets. He wheedled loans out of local banks to pay the troops. In a matter of weeks he had earned the respect of his soldiers with fairness, discipline, and thorough training. As one officer wrote, "He put on his general's hat and seemed to have grown two feet."

Unlike most generals, Bonaparte spoke frankly to his troops and shared in their hardships. No job was too small for him to undertake himself. The general even cleaned out cannon barrels, a task usually left to lowly corporals. His grateful soldiers started referring to him fondly as the "Little Corporal."

Bonaparte also proved to be a true military genius. Traditionally, battles were fought by armies that fired at each other while arranged in long, orderly lines. But Bonaparte broke with this tradition. Before a battle began, his spies searched out the weakest point of his opponent's line. Bonaparte would attack that point with overwhelming force and split the enemy's line into two parts. Then he'd order a small group of soldiers to dig defensive trenches in the gap. While they held off one half of the opposing army, Bonaparte destroyed the other half. Then he'd turn his whole army on what was left of his enemy.

In April, Bonaparte led his men into northern Italy, eager to show the world what he could do on the battlefield. At the time, Italy was not a unified country but a collection of separate states, many of which were ruled by Austria. Bonaparte invaded the westernmost state, the Kingdom of Piedmont, where Austrian and Italian troops awaited him.

According to plan, Bonaparte found a gap between the Austrians and the Italians. He split the enemy forces in half and forced the Austrians to retreat. Then he turned and knocked the Italians out of the war in one decisive battle.

With his flank no longer threatened, Bonaparte chased the Austrians toward the city of Milan. He caught up with them at the Adda River, near the little Italian town of Lodi.

On the afternoon of May 10, Bonaparte took his spyglass and went to investigate. The Austrians had taken up a position on the far side of the Adda River.

AT THE BATTLE OF LODI, Bonaparte proved he was a brilliant motivator. His loyal troops charged across a long, narrow bridge while exposed to heavy enemy fire.

There was only one bridge leading across it, and it was guarded by 12,000 Austrians armed with 16 large artillery guns. No commander would order his men to attack such a well-defended position. It was suicide.

But it had to be done.

Bonaparte assembled his troops and began to insult them, telling them they were too cowardly to take the bridge. He worked them into a rage and then turned them loose while the fife-and-drum corps played the *Marseillaise*, the French national anthem.

Despite withering fire from the Austrian artillery, his men took the bridge, the guns, and nearly 2,000 prisoners. The Austrians fled, leaving most of northern Italy to Bonaparte and his victorious army.

The Battle of Lodi was a turning point in Bonaparte's career, and he knew it. "It was only on the evening of Lodi that I believed myself a superior man," he later wrote. "I no longer saw myself as a mere general, but as a man called upon to influence the destiny of a people."

Chapter 7

Into Egypt

The "most delightful"
time of Bonaparte's life proves
FATAL TO HIS MEN.

BONAPARTE WAS NOT JUST BOASTING when he claimed to be more than a general. His conquest of northern Italy had made him one of the most powerful men in Europe, and he spent the next year and a half proving it.

From his base in Milan, Bonaparte marched to within 100 miles of Vienna and forced Austria into signing a peace treaty. He announced that he had "liberated" the Italians from Austrian rule. Then he proceeded to occupy Italy's greatest cities and send countless art treasures back to France. Finally, without authorization from his superiors, he created a new country, the Cisalpine Republic, from the Italian territories he had seized from Austria.

While he single-handedly transformed Italy, Bonaparte made sure that the people of France knew about his triumphs. He hired artists to create paintings of himself in heroic poses on the battlefield. He published his own newspapers and even wrote some of the articles himself. "Bonaparte flies like lightning and strikes like a thunderbolt," he boasted.

At the end of 1797, Bonaparte returned to France to see what he could make of his newly won fame. Publicly, the political leaders in Paris greeted him as a conquering hero. Privately, they weren't so admiring. Five men now held power in France as members of an executive body known as the Directory. They wondered just when this cocky young general would decide to use his loyal troops to kick them out of office and seize power for himself.

No doubt the directors were pleased when the returning hero accepted a mission that would take him far away to a dangerous and unfamiliar land. Bonaparte was going to Egypt, determined to seize the ancient kingdom for France.

Damaging Britain, however, was the expedition's true goal. For two centuries, British merchants had grown rich through trade with overseas colonies in India and the Americas. If the French conquered Egypt, they could establish a money-making colony of their own and then use it as a base to attack British interests in India.

The invasion began well. At 3 A.M. on July 1, 1798, Bonaparte led his army ashore in the great trade center of Alexandria. By lunchtime he had occupied the city.

But the hostile landscape of a foreign land began to wear the French down. They set off across the desert for Cairo, the Egyptian capital, hoping to find food and water as they marched. Sandstorms tore the flesh from their faces and glued their eyes shut with pockets of pus. Half-crazed from thirst, men drank

BONAPARTE AND HIS MEN struggle across the brutal
Egyptian desert.

from streams that were teeming with tiny leeches. Once
ingested, the leeches attached themselves to the inside
of the throat and grew until they choked their hosts
to death.

After defeating an Egyptian army at the Battle of
the Pyramids, the French marched into Cairo on July 24.
But Cairo was a terrible disappointment. Instead of the
treasure Bonaparte had promised his men, they found a

THE FRENCH ROUT an Egyptian army at the
Battle of the Pyramids. Bonaparte invented a new tactic
during this battle. He arranged his infantry in squares
to fight off the enemies' charging cavalry.

run-down city infested with rats and wild dogs. Even food
was hard to come by—the Egyptians seemed to live on a
diet of pumpkins, camel cheese, dry bread, and dates.

To make matters worse, the invaders soon learned
that they would be staying in Egypt longer than they

had planned. On August 1, the British navy destroyed the fleet that Bonaparte had left at anchor in Alexandria. Not only had the French lost their ride home, British ships were now blockading the Egyptian coast, keeping supplies and reinforcements from reaching the shore. Bonaparte and his men were stranded.

His escape route cut off, Bonaparte commandeered palaces in Cairo for himself and his officers. Then he set to work remaking Egypt in the image of France. He established a postal service, street lighting, a mint, a hospital, and regular stagecoach service between Cairo and Alexandria. He set up the first Arabic printing press and published books on modern medicine. He built windmills to pump water and grind grain.

To his fury, the Egyptians did not seem grateful. Bonaparte lost 250 men putting down a revolt in October. In February 1799, he marched his army up the Mediterranean shore to Syria, hoping to make "the whole of the coast friendly through war and negotiation."

Bonaparte promised his soldiers glory and riches, but all they found were more deserts, more fighting, and something even worse: the bubonic plague. Soon men were dying so fast that Bonaparte had to order a retreat back to Egypt.

In Cairo, the general received his first news from Europe since the British had destroyed his fleet six months earlier. None of it was good.

The British, still determined to destroy the French Republic, had persuaded the Turks, the Austrians, the Italians, and the Russians to form a second coalition against France. Under a renewed assault by the Austrians, the French had lost all the territory Bonaparte won for them in Italy. Their economy was on the verge of collapse.

Bonaparte was certain he was the only man who had the ability to save France. On August 23, his starving, sunburned, disease-racked army awoke to discover that their commander had slipped away in the night, bound for Paris with a few of his aides.

THE BRITISH NAVY DESTROYS French battleships anchored in Alexandria. Bonaparte managed to escape back to France, but he abandoned his plague-stricken troops in Egypt.

Bonaparte always remembered his 14 months in Egypt as "the most delightful of my life. In Egypt I found myself free from the wearisome restraints of civilization. I dreamed all sorts of things, and saw how all that I dreamed might be realized."

For the soldiers whom he abandoned without warning, Egypt was no idyllic dream, but a terrifying nightmare. They would remain trapped there until they surrendered to the British in 1801.

Uncovering Egypt

BONAPARTE'S INVASION OF EGYPT WAS MORE than a military exercise. The general intended to carry the secrets of one of the world's oldest civilizations back to France. To that end, he stocked his ships with more than 150 of France's finest mathematicians, scientists, and artists.

Despite facing many hardships, Bonaparte's scholars explored and documented ancient tombs at Thebes, Luxor, and Karnak. Most importantly, they discovered the Rosetta Stone, a rock slab with a 2,000-year-old decree written in three languages. The stone included Greek, everyday Egyptian script, and the ancient hieroglyphics used for sacred purposes.

The Rosetta Stone helped scholars decode the hieroglyphics of the ancient Egyptians, which no one—not even modern Egyptians— had understood for centuries.

THE ROSETTA STONE

CHAPTER 8

Seizing Power

BONAPARTE BOUNCES BACK
from his Egyptian disaster.

IT TOOK BONAPARTE AND HIS AIDES SIX weeks to sail from Egypt across the Mediterranean. They spent most of that time anxiously scanning the horizon for the masts of British ships patrolling the waters.

The people of France awaited Bonaparte's return with great excitement. Whenever he could get a ship past the British blockade, the general had sent home glowing reports of his conquests. As a result, most Parisians had no idea what a disaster the campaign had really been. Instead, they bought paintings of Egyptian palm trees from street vendors and attended theater spectacles that re-enacted the "Victory of the Pyramids." After all, the great general himself insisted he had "left Egypt well organized . . . and the Nile more beautiful than it has been in the last 50 years."

As Bonaparte's secretary later wrote, "He never hesitated to disguise the truth when he could make it embellish his own glory. He considered it sheer stupidity not to do so."

Thanks to his well-placed lies, Bonaparte returned home to wild acclaim. Cannon fire boomed in Paris to announce his landing in the south of France. Military bands oompahed through the streets of the capital. Theater performances were interrupted so the audiences could sing patriotic songs.

Tired of ten years of war and revolution, the people of France craved everything that this brilliant young general seemed to stand for: order, discipline, and the ability to get things done.

Bonaparte was eager to turn his popularity into real power. But first, he had personal business to attend to.

Shortly after Bonaparte's arrival in Egypt, an aide had broken the news that Josephine had taken a lover. Devastated, Bonaparte had pursued an affair of his own. But nothing could deaden the pain of his wife's betrayal. He decided he wanted to divorce the woman who had humiliated him.

After the two met in Paris in October 1799, Bonaparte locked himself in his room and refused to see her. Josephine knelt outside the door and wept, begging his forgiveness. She even sent her children to plead her case.

Eventually Bonaparte backed down, but something inside him had hardened. "I love no one," he wrote. "I know I have no true friends." From that moment on, nothing mattered to him except power.

It was an open secret that the Directory that ruled France was on the verge of collapse. It had lost both Italy and Belgium in recent months, and its war-torn economy had sunk into chaos. Bread riots and violent protests disturbed the peace all across France.

Napoleon met with his brother Lucien—who was now the president of the French legislature—and several other leaders. The group secretly decided that it was time to seize power.

On November 10, Bonaparte strode into the legislature in full army dress, surrounded by officers. He announced that he had come to save the republic from traitors who were funded by the British.

He was immediately surrounded by angry deputies who suspected that the most powerful general in France was out to destroy the republic, not save it. They beat Bonaparte with their fists until four guards hustled the general out of the room.

Once outside, surrounded by loyal troops and with his brother at his side, Bonaparte recovered himself. "I wanted to speak to them, and they met me with daggers!" he roared. His outraged soldiers stormed the building while terrified legislators escaped through the windows.

BONAPARTE WAS THREATENED by angry politicians after he took steps to overthrow the government. He was saved by his brother Lucien, who called in troops to disperse the crowd.

Later that night, legislators friendly to the Bonapartes voted to dissolve the Directory. They replaced it with three executives, called consuls, the most powerful of whom would soon be none other than Napoleon Bonaparte.

A jubilant Bonaparte promised to protect the ideals of the republic while bringing the chaos of the revolution to an end. "The Revolution is over," he proclaimed. "I am the Revolution."

CHAPTER 9

Enforcing the Peace

NAPOLEON BECOMES KING in all but name.

THE GOAL OF THE FRENCH REVOLUTION had been to replace France's all-powerful king with a government that gave its citizens "liberty, equality, and fraternity." Bonaparte supported the ideal of equality—fair, predictable laws that protected the rights of citizens. He also recognized the value of fraternity—a sense of patriotism and national identity. But ten years of revolution had convinced him that liberty was overrated. In his view, when people were free to do what they liked, the world became a disordered and inefficient place.

"I had been nourished by reflecting on liberty," he said, "but I thrust it aside when it obstructed my path."

Bonaparte's first act as consul was to compose a new constitution that would give him tight control over France. The constitution allowed the First Consul—which was to be Bonaparte himself—to propose all laws and appoint all government officials. The Second and Third Consuls were demoted to advisers.

When the constitution was ready, the new leaders sent it to the people for a vote. They announced the final tally with a straight face, although it had obviously been fixed: three million for, 1,562 against.

Bonaparte was now king in all but name. In February 1800, he and Josephine took up residence in the Tuileries Palace, the former home of the French kings. Because kings were known by their first names,

AFTER OVERTHROWING THE DIRECTORY, Bonaparte (center) moved quickly to seize power from France's two other consuls— Roger Ducos (left) and Emmanuel Joseph Sieyès (right).

Bonaparte began to refer to himself as "Napoleon," even though he had never liked the name.

Now that he had a country to govern, Napoleon wanted to bring an end to the decade of wars that had drained France's resources. The Austrians had driven France out of the Italian territories that Napoleon had "liberated" four years earlier. But a surprise attack in Italy, Napoleon reasoned, might knock Austria out of the war and convince the British to negotiate a final peace.

So on May 15, Napoleon launched one of the most daring invasions the world has ever known. He marched his men over the Alps from France into Italy.

The Alps are the tallest mountains in Europe. Their snow-covered, windswept peaks rise to 15,000 feet and are forbidding even in summer.

Only one army had ever crossed that barrier— Hannibal's Carthaginians, more than 2,000 years earlier. Unlike the Carthaginians, the French had heavy iron cannons they'd have to drag with them. It simply wasn't possible.

But, as Napoleon liked to say, *impossible* wasn't a French word. He had his men hollow out fallen trees to make sleds. They disassembled the cannons, packed the parts into the sleds, and dragged the awkward loads through the narrow mountain passes. In just five days, the French army crossed the mountains into Italy.

Napoleon's scouts reported that the Austrians, startled by the sudden appearance of the French, were preparing to retreat. But on the morning of June 14, the Austrians launched their own surprise attack near the little Italian town of Marengo. By lunchtime, the Austrians were so sure they had won that their commanding officer left the battlefield.

Just then, however, one of Napoleon's generals appeared with reinforcements. "This battle is completely lost," the general told Napoleon, "but it is only two o'clock. There is time to win another."

Napoleon mounted a fierce bombardment with 18 artillery guns, and then finished the Austrians off with a cavalry charge. Within 24 hours, the Austrians had agreed to withdraw from Italy. Both Austria and Britain sued for peace. For the first time in more than ten years, France was not fighting for its survival.

To no one's surprise, the people of France showed their gratitude by voting Napoleon First Consul for Life. This time the margin was 3,572,329 to 2,569. Few people had the courage to point out that Napoleon's brother Lucien had supervised the counting.

NAPOLEON'S MEN DRAG THEIR CANNONS over the Alps
in May 1800. No military force had dared to make this invasion
since the Carthaginian leader Hannibal took his army and
elephants across in 218 B.C.

CHAPTER 10

Remaking France

The First Consul works to
BRING ORDER
TO FRANCE.

WITH THE WAR OUT OF THE WAY, Napoleon concentrated on building a new nation. According to the ambassador from Prussia, who met with Napoleon early in 1802, the French ruler claimed to be finished with war. Instead, the ambassador reported, the First Consul was full of plans for "canals to be completed and opened, roads to be made or repaired, harbors to be dredged, towns to be embellished, places of worship and religious establishments to be endowed, public instruction . . . to be provided for."

Napoleon had always loved the excitement of new plans and projects. Now he threw himself into reforming the French government with the same energy and eye for detail he had shown on the battlefield.

"I was born and made for work," he said, and it was true.

Napoleon needed very little sleep and had a photographic memory for print. He liked to keep his life tidy and organized. "Different subjects and different affairs are arranged in my head as in a cupboard," he wrote. "When I wish to interrupt one train of thought, I shut that drawer and open another. Do I wish to sleep? I simply close all the drawers and there I am—asleep."

His obsession with efficiency extended even to meal times. He left the table after five minutes at breakfast, eight minutes at lunch, and 20 minutes at dinner, even in the middle of conversations.

After years of poverty, however, Napoleon took great pleasure in the luxuries available to a powerful leader. He began the day at 6 A.M. with an hour-long bath to soothe his chronic skin problems. He had servants dress and shave him while secretaries read the newspapers aloud.

Then the day's work really began. Napoleon could read almost as fast as he could turn pages, and he was curious about everything. He badgered everyone he met with streams of questions—although he was often too impatient to wait for their answers. He demanded that his men work as hard as he did. Late one night he noticed that the members of his Council of State were beginning to droop. "Let's keep awake, citizens," he urged. "It's only two o'clock. We must earn our salaries!"

He worked so hard because he believed that "a new government must dazzle." And his did. The reforms he put in place between 1800 and 1804 have remained among the most enduring and influential the world has ever known.

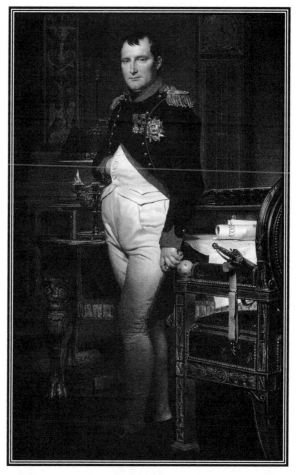

NAPOLEON POSES IN HIS OFFICE at the Tuileries Palace.
Once in power, he was determined to rebuild France. He revised
France's legal and education systems, built roads, and raised cash
by selling the vast Louisiana Territory to the United States.

Napoleon knew that his success would depend on having the support of as many people as possible. As he said, "Public opinion is the thermometer a monarch should constantly consult."

So instead of using his power to punish his enemies, he worked to make France welcoming to everyone from Royalists to radical revolutionaries. In 1801, he signed a treaty with Pope Pius VII that repaired France's relationship with the Catholic Church.

Napoleon tried to make education available to everyone, regardless of their social rank or income level. He opened a network of public schools and teacher's colleges and even wrote some of the textbooks himself—with a little help from university scholars.

He also wanted the French to be prosperous. He slashed taxes and balanced the government's budget. He built signal towers that could pass coded messages quickly between cities. He dug canals, paved roads, installed aqueducts for clean water, and improved sewer systems.

His most important reform, however, was the Napoleonic Code, a law code that is still the foundation of many of the world's legal systems. When he assumed power, the French legal system was a mess. It was full of exemptions and special privileges, and it varied from place to place.

Napoleon's new code was written in clear and easy-to-understand language. It tried to make relationships between people and their neighbors, family members, and property predictable and fair. For the first time, the same laws applied to everyone in exactly the same way—everyone, that is, who happened to be male. Napoleon believed that "women are nothing but machines for producing children." Under his government, fathers and husbands had almost total power over their children and wives. Despite its flaws, however, the Napoleonic Code was by far the fairest of Europe's legal systems.

Napoleon Bonaparte in Pictures

WAR GAMES
When Napoleon was nine, his father sent him to a military school in France. The young Corsican disliked France but loved activities related to war, including snowball fights.

HEAD OF STATE
In 1789, France was torn apart by a revolution. Thousands of people were executed by the guillotine, including former king Louis XVI, whose severed head is shown here.

HIRED GUN
When Napoleon was just 24, he was chosen to seize the seaport of Toulon from the Royalists and their British allies.

DIRTY WORK

In 1795, thousands of Royalists rose up against the revolutionary government. Napoleon crushed the revolt by firing into the mostly unarmed crowd.

CORSICAN SAVAGE

As a young man, Napoleon (left) was passionate, curious, and ambitious. He was also very awkward in social situations.

LOVE AND WAR

In 1796, Napoleon married Rose de Beauharnais, whom he insisted on calling Josephine.

LATER, GUYS
Napoleon's invasion of
Egypt was a disaster for
his troops, who were
devastated by the plague.
In 1799, Napoleon
abandoned them.

SELF PROMOTION
After becoming First Consul of
France, Napoleon crossed the
Alps to invade Italy. He later had
this painting made to celebrate
his victories.

78

THE EMPRESS
After Napoleon crowned himself and Josephine emperor and empress of France, he asked artist Jacques Louis David to paint the ceremony.

MASTER OF EUROPE
Soldiers cheer Napoleon after his victory at Austerlitz, which crushed Europe's third coalition to destroy France.

MONUMENTAL EGO

In 1806, Napoleon commissioned the Arc de Triomphe to celebrate his victories at Austerlitz and other battles.

POWER HUNGRY

According to this British political cartoon from 1803, Napoleon intended to swallow the whole world.

A STUMBLE IN SPAIN

In 1807, Napoleon launched a disastrous campaign against Spain. In this cartoon, he is depicted as a defeated bullfighter; the bull represents Spain.

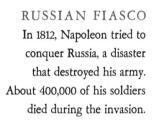

YOUNG ROYALTY

In 1810 Napoleon married Marie-Louise, the young daughter of Austria's emperor. One year later, she gave birth to Napoleon's heir, Napoleon II.

RUSSIAN FIASCO

In 1812, Napoleon tried to conquer Russia, a disaster that destroyed his army. About 400,000 of his soldiers died during the invasion.

LONELY END

After escaping from exile in 1815, Napoleon was defeated at Waterloo and imprisoned on St. Helena, a tiny island in the south Atlantic Ocean. He died there six years later, calling for Josephine.

PART 3

Emperor Napoleon

Better than King

With a little help
from his friends, Napoleon
CROWNS HIMSELF EMPEROR.

December 2, 1804, dawned cold and gray. Snow had fallen during the night, and the cobblestone roads leading into the heart of Paris were slick with muddy slush. Inside the soaring stone vaults of Notre Dame cathedral, Europe's greatest figures shivered in their silks and jewels. They had been waiting for Napoleon for hours.

It was unlike him to be late, but he had taken his time all morning, wanting to savor every delicious moment. Finally, when every inch of him was bathed, perfumed, and swathed in diamonds, silks, and furs, he pulled his brother Joseph in front of a mirror.

"What would Dad think if he could see us now?" he preened.

As he and Josephine finally pulled up to Notre Dame in their gold-and-crystal carriage, a thin ray of sunlight broke through the clouds. Napoleon was sure it was a good omen.

He strode briskly into the cathedral, whose forbidding stone expanse was decorated almost past recognition. At the end of the carpeted aisle, Pope Pius VII waited to anoint him emperor, heir to the great ninth-century ruler Charlemagne.

Charlemagne had been crowned by the pope, but Napoleon had no intention of receiving his crown from anyone. Instead he grasped the jeweled crown in his small, plump hands and set it firmly on his own head.

Having won the glittering prize, he was determined to keep it. "Power is my mistress," he reflected after the

IN 1804, NAPOLEON ENDED the French Republic by
crowning himself emperor. He wore a golden laurel wreath
similar to those worn by the emperors of ancient Rome.

coronation. "I have worked too hard at her conquest to
allow anyone to take her away from me now."

Napoleon set out to protect his hard-won position
by building a network of secret police and government
spies. It was their job to root out dissent in all corners
of France. Anyone foolish enough to criticize the

new emperor in print was likely to find his press destroyed and himself in prison or in exile. "Four hostile newspapers are more to be feared than a thousand bayonets," Napoleon wrote.

Napoleon appointed the ruthless Joseph Fouché to oversee the empire's network of spies. Every morning, Fouché and his staff distilled their reports into the *Bulletin de la Police* (Police Bulletin), which was then printed and presented to the emperor.

According to one of Napoleon's close advisers, Fouché had "a heart as hard as diamond, a stomach of iron, and a tearless eye."

Napoleon once returned from a battle and asked Fouché, "What would you have done if I had just been killed?"

"Sire, I would have seized as much power for myself as I possibly could, so as not to have become the victim of events," Fouché answered instantly.

Napoleon laughed and shouted, "Splendid! That's the way to play the game!"

Unlimited Power

Napoleon decides to
CONQUER THE WORLD.

BEFORE BECOMING EMPEROR, NAPOLEON fought wars to defend France against her enemies. By 1804, his intentions had changed. "I wanted to rule the world, and in order to do this I needed unlimited power," he explained near the end of his career.

That was bad news for France's neighbors, especially Britain. The tiny island nation was half the size of France and had only a third as many people. Its army of 250,000 was dwarfed by France's 1.5 million troops. The channel that divided the two countries was only 20

NAPOLEON (with spyglass) watches while his Army of England performs military exercises in the English Channel.

miles wide at its narrowest point. Hoping to conquer his enemy, Napoleon assembled a 150,000-man invasion force, called the Army of England. He built a huge fleet of barges that would carry it across the channel.

Rather than wait for the French to strike first, the British had declared war again in 1803. The powerful British navy took up positions along the coast of France, forming a blockade to keep French ships safely in port. By the spring of 1805, they had persuaded Austria and Russia to join a new coalition against France.

Napoleon had no intention of being bullied. He drew Spain into an alliance and ordered French warships to the Spanish coast, where reinforcements waited. The combined Franco-Spanish fleet would pretend to sail to British colonies in the Caribbean. When the British pursued them, the ships would secretly double back to support an invasion of Britain.

His admirals protested, insisting that the winds would keep the French fleet from eluding the British. Napoleon ignored them. His armies had overcome the burning sands of Egypt and the driving snow of the Alps. Surely his navy could overlook a few puffs of wind.

With his naval plan underway, Napoleon turned his attention to Austria. Determined to strike before the Russian army had time to join its Austrian allies, he donned his general's uniform and sprung into action. He marched his Grand Army 300 miles to the Rhine River in quick-time—120 steps a minute. His men pressed ahead day and night with one ten-minute break every two hours, all while carrying 60-pound packs on their backs.

No one had any idea that an army could move so quickly. In September 1805, Napoleon crossed the Rhine and defeated the surprised Austrians at the Battle of Ulm. He surrounded Vienna before anyone realized what was happening. The Austrian capital surrendered without a shot.

After a brief rest, Napoleon pushed his troops east, toward the Russians.

On December 2, Napoleon met the Austro-Russian army led by Francis I and Alexander I in the cold mist at Austerlitz. With his decisive strike at the center of the enemy line, the French emperor won the greatest victory of his career.

Just a few days earlier, however, Napoleon had received news of a crippling defeat. On October 21, the British navy had caught up with the Franco-Spanish fleet near Spain's Cape Trafalgar in the Mediterranean Sea. Just before battle began, the British commander, Admiral Horatio Nelson, sent a signal to his fleet: "England expects that every man will do his duty."

THE HMS *VICTORY* pounds a French battleship to splinters
during the Battle of Trafalgar. Napoleon's fleet was almost completely
destroyed, dooming his plan to invade the island of Britain.

Nelson lost his life to a French musket ball that day.
But his sailors did their duty—and more. Within a few
hours, half of Napoleon's ships were sunk and the rest
were in full retreat.

The French navy never recovered from its defeat
at Trafalgar. Napoleon was forced to scrap his plan to
invade Britain once and for all.

C H A P T E R   1 3

The Continental System

Napoleon plots to STARVE THE BRITISH INTO SUBMISSION.

WITH THEIR VICTORY AT TRAFALGAR, the British had eluded Napoleon's grasp. The rest of Europe, however, lay in the emperor's palm. After Ulm and Austerlitz, Napoleon seemed unstoppable.

In the fall of 1806, the rulers of Prussia decided they could no longer ignore the French army, which had taken up quarters on their southern border. "The idea that Prussia could take the field against me by herself seems so ridiculous that it does not merit discussion," scoffed Napoleon.

In October, 19 days after the Prussian army began to mobilize, Napoleon crushed it at the battles of Jena and Auerstedt, killing 140,000 enemy soldiers.

With Austria and Prussia out of the way, Napoleon turned his eye east toward Russia. After a brutal winter, he met Tsar Alexander's army on June 14, 1807, near the Russian border. The Battle of Friedland lasted 23 terrible hours before the Russians finally fled across the Lyna River in the dead of night.

While the dead were still being buried, Napoleon met Alexander on a raft in the center of the Lyna, which marked Russia's western boundary.

Alexander greeted him with the words, "Sir, I hate the English as much as you do."

Napoleon laughed and answered, "So I see we have made peace."

It was, from the Russian point of view, a generous peace. The French didn't ask for any Russian territory at

NAPOLEON (on white stallion) during his victory against Russia at Friedland. Tsar Alexander of Russia was forced to make peace with Napoleon after the battle.

all. What Napoleon wanted was an ally in his ongoing war against the British. And since his plan to invade the British Isles had been foiled, he would fight the war in the marketplace instead of on the battlefield.

The British had recently become Europe's greatest economic power. British factories powered by newly developed steam engines churned out textiles and manufactured goods of all kinds. A huge fleet of merchant ships traded these low-cost goods for luxuries around the world.

Napoleon planned to attack the British where it would hurt the most—in their pocketbooks. He wanted all the nations on the European mainland to stop trading with Britain. Any British merchant ship that tried to sell its wares in a European port would have its cargo seized.

If the plan worked, the British economy would crash. Unemployed workers would rise up and overthrow their king. At the very least, the British would be forced to sign a peace treaty favorable to France.

Napoleon called his boycott the "Continental System." He had already forced the Spanish, Prussians, and Austrians to participate. At the meeting on the Lyna, Alexander agreed to join the boycott as well.

Only tiny Portugal was left to persuade, and Napoleon's embargo of Britain would be complete.

CHAPTER 14

The Spanish Ulcer

Napoleon makes a
COSTLY MISCALCULATION.

By THE AUTUMN OF 1807, NAPOLEON'S
control of Europe seemed all but assured. He had
vanquished Austria, Prussia, and Russia. With the
help of these former enemies, it seemed only a matter
of time until the Continental System starved Britain
into submission.

Napoleon was at the very peak of his career. All of
Europe lay at his feet. And yet, his spirits were low. He
had suffered from a skin disease ever since the Battle of
Toulon, and some days the itching was enough to drive

him mad. Now his stomach was bothering him too. Little wonder, Josephine told him. It served him right for the way he crammed down his meals and refused to eat fruit or vegetables.

But Napoleon had more than just indigestion. He began to put on weight. He had trouble urinating. His skin, which had always been noticeably pale, became shiny pink. Children were heard to say that he looked like a pink porcelain pig.

The emperor's temper, never good at the best of times, was worse than ever. He threw things and called even his most loyal advisers terrible names. In the early years, he had been friendly and curious. Now he didn't want to hear anything but approval.

He worried constantly about betrayal, perhaps because he himself had betrayed so many people. As he admitted, "I like only those people who are useful to me, and then only as long as they are useful."

Napoleon soothed his fears by giving power to the only people he trusted—his family members. He made his older brother, Joseph, king of Naples and Sicily in southern Italy. His younger brother Louis took the Dutch crown. Napoleon created the Kingdom of Westphalia from several German states and gave it to his brother Jerome. His sister Elisa became grand duchess of Tuscany in northern Italy.

But no matter how much of Europe he handed out to his family, Napoleon could not seem to keep British goods out of the continent. Merchants all over Europe ignored the blockade and secretly welcomed British ships into their ports. Some of the worst offenders could be found in Spain and Portugal, whose combined 1,600 miles of coastline were nearly impossible to police.

Late in 1807, Napoleon decided he had to try. French troops invaded Portugal from bases inside Spain, forcing the Portuguese royal family into flight.

The following spring Napoleon cracked down on Spain. He invited the entire Spanish royal family for a state visit to Paris—and then placed them under arrest. With an empty throne now available, he persuaded his brother Joseph to trade in his Italian crowns and become Spain's next king.

The Spanish people, however, did not welcome the Bonapartes. Instead, they rose up in rebellion against their new French masters.

THIS PAINTING—*Third of May, 1808*, by Francisco Goya—shows a French firing squad preparing to kill a group of Spanish rebels. The French army massacred hundreds of Spaniards on this date.

For the first time in his military career, Napoleon seemed overmatched. The Spanish didn't fight the kind of organized battles he had learned to dominate. Instead, they waged a guerrilla war—ambushing a small party of French troops here, slitting a drunken soldier's throat there, poisoning a well somewhere else. They refused to show themselves yet seemed to turn up everywhere.

Suddenly, Napoleon watched his fearsome French army grow hungry and frightened, losing a hundred men a day. In his younger days, Napoleon would probably have realized that the situation was hopeless. But there had been too many successes. He now believed that great leaders should "never retreat, never retract . . . never admit a mistake."

And so the Peninsular War—the "Spanish ulcer," as he called it—lingered on. It drained wealth, strength, and hope from Napoleon's followers, month after frustrating month, year after desperate year.

CHAPTER 15

Domestic Affairs

Napoleon decides he NEEDS AN HEIR.

NAPOLEON CELEBRATED HIS FORTIETH birthday on August 15, 1809. He had accomplished more than anyone would have believed possible, defeating the most powerful armies in the world and placing much of Europe under his control.

But something was missing. What would happen to his vast empire after he was gone? He had been married for 13 years and he still had no heir to carry his name into the future. It was a situation he could no longer tolerate.

Just before Christmas in 1809, Napoleon met with Josephine and explained that he was divorcing her "for the good of France." A few minutes later, guards heard bloodcurdling screams. Then the emperor shouted for help—Josephine had fainted and he could not revive her.

Napoleon carried her to her rooms himself, shocked and a little pleased by her reaction. He promised that they would still see each other and that he would continue to support her financially. "God alone knows what this resolve has cost my heart," he assured her. But his country needed an heir.

JOSEPHINE FAINTS after Napoleon announces his plan to divorce her. At their divorce ceremony, Josephine was forced to read this: "I must declare that . . . [I have] no hope of bearing children who would fulfill the needs of [my husband's] policies."

A few weeks later, Napoleon ended the marriage with a ceremony conducted in front of 450 guests. When it was over he told his aides that he was looking for a suitable "womb."

Napoleon quickly found one in the 19-year-old Austrian princess Marie-Louise. She was the daughter of his former enemy Francis I, the emperor whose army Napoleon had vanquished at Austerlitz. Marie-Louise's mother had borne 13 children; her grandmother had borne 18. Given her family history, Napoleon thought his prospects for an heir looked good.

Marie-Louise required some persuading before agreeing to the match. Told as a child that Napoleon was a devil, she had invented a vengeful game involving her future suitor. She named dolls after him and roasted them in the "Hell" of her nursery fireplace.

But times had changed since then. Her father, eager to ensure a continued peace with France, assured Marie-Louise that the marriage was God's will.

In the spring of 1810, Napoleon and Marie-Louise were married in Paris. To the surprise of everyone, the marriage was a success. Napoleon was determined to charm his young bride, and he succeeded. She honestly grew to love the man whose effigies she had thrown gleefully in the fire. Napoleon, in turn, was charmed by his young wife's liveliness and youthful innocence.

Less than a year later, Marie-Louise gave birth to a son. He was immediately christened Napoleon II. For good measure, Napoleon named him King of Rome.

NAPOLEON AND MARIE-LOUISE (far right) with their son, the infant King of Rome. Marie-Louise was just 19 when her father, Francis I of Austria, asked her to marry the 40-year-old emperor.

CHAPTER 16

৽৽৽৽৽৽৽৽৽৽৽৽৽৽৽

Disaster on the Battlefield

Napoleon's army STARVES IN THE RUSSIAN SNOW.

Napoleon's private life may have been happy, but his economic war against Britain was breaking down. Too many rulers turned a blind eye to smugglers who brought low-priced British goods into Europe.

Tsar Alexander of Russia, for one, was convinced that the price of friendship with France was too high. Russia was a poor country that needed Britain's help to modernize. On December 31, 1810, the tsar announced that Russia would resume trade with Great Britain.

Napoleon was furious. In the past, shrewd advisers like Fouché would have listened to him rant and then talked him out of doing anything reckless. But many of the emperor's closest aides had resigned. There was no one left with the experience and the courage to point out that no man could possibly control the entire continent.

So, in the spring of 1812, the largest army the world had ever known began to make its slow and lumbering way from Paris to Russia. Napoleon was determined to force the tsar back into the Continental System.

In the past, Napoleon had always won his battles by moving faster and acting more boldly than his opponents. But an army of 600,000 cannot do anything quickly. The daily food ration alone required more than 6,000 wagons. Each of those wagons needed horses to pull it. So did the heavy cannons of the emperor's beloved artillery. A little rain and the entire army got stuck in the mud for days.

According to Napoleon, "the great proof of madness is the disproportion of one's designs to one's means." He meant that anyone who tried to execute a wildly ambitious plan without the resources to succeed was insane. And by his own definition, the invasion of Russia proved that he had lost his mind.

Napoleon initially set aside a single month for his conquest of Russia. He was certain the war was his to win if he could just maneuver the Russian army into a decisive battle. But the Russians refused to fight. They retreated before Napoleon's clumsy advance, destroying food supplies and poisoning wells as they went.

Napoleon lost hundreds of men to illness or desertion every day. Their starving horses ate unripe grain and thatch from cottage roofs. Soon thousands of pack animals were rotting under the sun in the army's wake. The invasion had become what one historian would call "the longest traffic jam in European history."

When Napoleon finally caught up with the Russians, things went from bad to worse. On September 7, he attacked the Russian army near the village of Borodino, two days' march from Moscow. The Russians suffered 40,000 casualties in a single day, but they refused to surrender. "These Russians let themselves be killed as if they were not men, but mere machines," Napoleon marveled.

The next morning, the French woke to discover— nothing. The Russians had stolen away in the night, and taken their supplies with them.

Baffled, the French pressed on to Moscow and the hot food and treasure that awaited. They arrived to find treasure, but little else. The city had been abandoned. "Moscow appeared to be lost in deep sleep," one of Napoleon's aides remembered.

Someone must have been there, however, because that night a fire broke out—then another, and another. The Russians were burning their own city to the ground. Soon 80 percent of Moscow had gone up in smoke.

Faced with starvation, Napoleon finally ordered a retreat. The ragged remains of his army headed west from Moscow, leaving wagons and cannons behind as

THE FRENCH WATCH as Moscow burns. Napoleon had expected Alexander to bargain for peace, as other monarchs had done. He wrote to the tsar: "Beautiful, magical Moscow exists no more. How could you destroy the loveliest city in the world?"

they fled. Five out of every six soldiers who had followed Napoleon into Russia that year did not return home.

In December, Napoleon abandoned the remains of his army, creeping away disguised as a servant.

Napoleon would fight on, but his once-fearsome army had been devastated. Armies from all across Europe joined forces for a final push to destroy the French Empire. On October 18, 1813, at the Battle of

Nations, 400,000 troops from Russia, Britain, Prussia, and Sweden defeated a French army that was less than half that size. Then they crossed the French border and marched toward Paris.

On January 25, 1814, Napoleon kissed Marie-Louise and their three-year-old son good-bye and prepared to defend what was left of his empire. For the next two months, he fought with some of his old brilliance, but it was too late. There was nothing left——no more soldiers, horses, ammunition, or food.

The emperor finally surrendered on April 11, 1814, nearly two weeks after Paris had fallen to his enemies. The next morning he uncorked a small vial of poison he'd carried for years and swallowed its contents. He broke into a sweat, writhed in agony, and began to vomit. But the poison had lost some of its potency, and to his disappointment, he survived.

The rulers of Europe, meanwhile, were done with Napoleon. They allowed him to keep the title of emperor but exiled him to Elba, a small

NAPOLEON REACTS to the news that the combined
armies of the sixth coalition had taken Paris. Even
Napoleon's father-in-law, Francis I of Austria, had joined
the war to remove Napoleon from power.

island just out of sight of Corsica. They gave the
French throne to Louis XVIII, brother of the king
who had been executed during the revolution.

Just a year earlier, Napoleon had reigned over 80
million people sprawled across half a continent. Now he
ruled a tiny island with a population of less than 25,000.

CHAPTER 17

Waterloo

Napoleon escapes from
exile but meets his fate on
A MUDDY BATTLEFIELD
IN BELGIUM.

On Elba, Napoleon settled into a small villa that would have to serve as a palace. He had been promised enough money to rebuild the villa and support the 1,000 troops he was allowed as an army. But the new French ruler, the fussy Louis XVIII, refused to pay a franc to the man who had stolen his family's throne.

Louis would pay dearly for holding a grudge.

Napoleon tried to be enthusiastic about his island empire. He designed a new flag for his country. He drew up plans to reform Elba's economy and its government. But without money, he could put none of his plans into action.

After nine months in exile, Napoleon decided to escape. On the night of February 26, 1815, he assembled a convoy of 700 men, seven ships, four big guns, and three generals. Silently, the escapees sailed into the open sea, right under the noses of the British navy. Three days later, Napoleon landed on French soil, commanding an army no bigger than the old French legislature.

Napoleon led his men north toward Paris. Their first test came a few miles south of Grenoble, where they were challenged by a battalion of Louis XVIII's troops. Napoleon dismounted and walked toward the hostile force. He opened the front of the lucky gray coat he had worn to every battle since Marengo and shouted, "It is I, Napoleon. Kill your emperor if you wish."

No one moved.

Deciding that was a good sign, Napoleon added a huge lie. "The 45 wisest men in the Paris government have summoned me from Elba. My return is backed by the three leading powers of Europe."

Again, no one moved.

Finally, the battalion threw their hats in the air and cheered, "Long live the emperor!"

On the first day of spring, Napoleon marched into Paris. His army had swelled with thousands of enthusiastic recruits, and no one opposed his return. The timid Louis XVIII had fled. A cheering crowd waited at the Tuileries Palace and insisted on carrying Napoleon the last few steps of his journey.

Napoleon's second honeymoon as emperor did not last long. The Russians, Austrians, Prussians, and Spanish united under British command and sent armies toward France's eastern border. Napoleon struck on June 15, long before anyone expected him to, and defeated a Prussian army on the Belgian border.

NAPOLEON (on horseback) gives orders during the Battle of Waterloo. This defeat would mark the end of his spectacular and bloody career.

The Duke of Wellington, commander of the coalition forces, heard the news while attending a ball in Brussels. "Napoleon has humbugged me!" he exclaimed.

But Napoleon had taught his enemies the importance of quick action. Wellington immediately called in his aides and disappeared into a side room with a map of southern Belgium to plan his counterattack.

Wellington moved into position near the Belgian town of Waterloo on June 17. A cold drizzle fell on the battlefield, recalling the day of Napoleon's triumph at Austerlitz. But the Battle of Waterloo would be no Austerlitz. It began at noon the next day and ended at nightfall with the French running for their lives.

Napoleon had several chances to deal Wellington a crushing blow, but he hesitated each time until the moment had passed. In the late afternoon a Prussian force of 50,000 soldiers arrived at the battlefield. They reinforced their exhausted British allies and forced the French into retreat. By the time the sun set, nearly 50,000 men lay dead on the battlefield.

After Waterloo, the kings of Europe took no chances with Napoleon. They exiled him to the tiny volcanic island of St. Helena in the south Atlantic. It was more than 700 miles from the closest land. A squadron of warships, a garrison of 2,250 men, and 500 cannons kept watch over the shoreline.

Napoleon spent six cold, damp, lonely years on St. Helena. He had been allowed a dozen servants and an equal number of aides, all of whom he quickly learned to despise. Josephine was dead, killed by a throat infection during his exile on Elba. Marie-Louise and their son languished under house arrest at the Schoenbrunn Palace in Vienna. The boy would die there of tuberculosis at the age of 21.

IN 1815, NAPOLEON WAS EXILED a second time—to St. Helena, 700 miles from the nearest bit of land. The fallen emperor would never see his wife or son again.

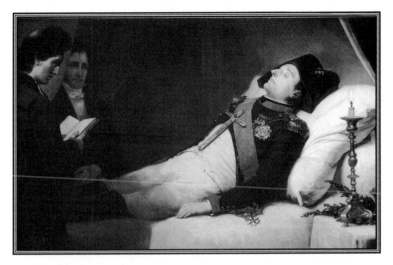

NAPOLEON ON HIS DEATHBED. Twenty years later, his body would be returned to Paris and given a massive funeral.

Napoleon's health was poor and soon got worse. He had difficulty going to the bathroom and suffered from terrible stomach pains. Convinced that he was being poisoned by British agents, he stopped eating. He died on May 5, 1821, calling for Josephine.

Wicked?

To the bitter end, Napoleon told himself and anyone who would listen that he was one of the great men of history. "I closed the gulf of anarchy and cleared the chaos, I purified the Revolution," he insisted.

Like most of his proclamations, these words are only partially true.

What is true is that he brought the chaos that was the French Revolution to an end. The revolutionaries had claimed to fight for "liberty, equality, and fraternity." It could be argued that Napoleon achieved two of those goals at the expense of the third.

Reforms like the Napoleonic Code made France a fairer, more egalitarian place. But no one could say that Napoleon made his people free. His secret police put political enemies in jail. He censored the press, reducing the number of newspapers in Paris from 60 to four by 1814.

Moreover, many of Napoleon's accomplishments proved temporary. As soon as Napoleon was gone, the people of Italy, Portugal, Spain, and the German states overthrew the corrupt rulers Napoleon had appointed. He even left France's borders smaller than when he had seized power.

As a general, Napoleon has few equals in history. When someone asked the Duke of Wellington to name the greatest military mind of the age, he answered, "In this age, in past ages, in any age, Napoleon." But the cost of his glory was almost incalculable. Six million people died in his wars. Tens of millions more lost their homes or their children.

Germaine de Staël, one of Napoleon's political rivals, summed up Napoleon's great flaw. "He regarded a human being as an action or a thing, and not as a fellow creature," she wrote. "He did not hate any more than he loved; for him nothing existed but himself."

Timeline of Terror

1769

1769: Napoleon Bonaparte is born in Ajaccio, Corsica, on August 15.

1778: Napoleon wins a scholarship to a military school in France.

1793: In the middle of the French Revolution, Napoleon wins fame by defeating Royalists in Toulon.

1795: Napoleon fires into a crowd of Royalist rebels to protect the revolutionary government in Paris.

1796: After marrying Josephine de Beauharnais, Napoleon goes off to defeat the Austrians in Italy.

1798: Napoleon leads a failed expedition to Egypt.

1799: Napoleon returns to France a hero and seizes power in a coup.

1804: Napoleon passes his Napoleonic Code and crowns himself emperor of France.

1805: The French navy is destroyed by the British at the Battle of Trafalgar. Six weeks later, Bonaparte defeats Russia and Austria at the Battle of Austerlitz.

1806: Napoleon defeats Prussia at the battles of Jena and Auerstedt.

1810: Napoleon marries Marie-Louise of Austria.

1811: Their son, Napoleon II, is born.

1812: Napoleon launches his disastrous invasion of Russia.

1813: The French are defeated by a coalition of troops from Austria, Britain, Prussia, Russia, and Sweden at the Battle of the Nations.

1814: Napoleon abdicates the French throne and is exiled to Elba.

1815: Napoleon returns to power, loses the Battle of Waterloo, and is exiled to St. Helena.

1821: Napoleon dies on St. Helena.

1821

aqueduct (AK-wuh-duhkt) *noun* a large bridge built to carry water

artillery (ar-TIL-uh-ree) *noun* large, powerful guns, such as cannons

battalion (buh-TAL-yun) *noun* a large unit of soldiers; in Napoleon's armies, a unit of about 840 soldiers

blockade (blok-ADE) *noun* the closing off of an area to keep people or supplies from moving in or out

bubonic plague (byoo-BON-ik PLAYG) *noun* a serious disease that spreads quickly and often causes death

cavalry (KAV-uhl-ree) *noun* soldiers who fight on horseback

coalition (koh-uh-LISH-uhn) *noun* a tempoary alliance

commission (kuh-MISH-uhn) *noun* a written order giving rank in the armed services

constitution (kon-stuh-TOO-shuhn) *noun* the system of laws in a country that state the rights of the people and the powers of the government

consul (KON-suhl) *noun* any of the three chief executives of France from 1799 to 1804; Napoleon was First Consul, the most important of the three

Directory (duh-REK-tuh-ree) *noun* the executive body, made up of five men, that led France from 1795 to 1799

dissent (di-SENT) *noun* disagreement with an opinion or idea

egotist (EE-goh-tist) *noun* someone who has an exaggerated sense of self importance

embargo (em-BAR-goh) *noun* an official ban on trade or other commercial activity with a particular country

envoy (ON-voy) *noun* a person appointed to represent one government in its dealings with another

exemption (eg-ZEMP-shun) *noun* a release from a rule that others have to follow exile (EG-zile) *noun* the state of being barred from one's native country

flank (FLANGK) *noun* the far left or right side of a group of soldiers

fraternity (fruh-TUR-nih-tee) *noun* the state or feeling of friendship and mutual support within a group

guerrilla (guh-RIL-uh) *adjective* describing a type of warfare in which small groups of fighters launch surprise attacks against an official army

guillotine (GEE-uh-teen) *noun* a large machine with a sharp blade used to sever the heads of criminals

hieroglyphics (hye-ur-uh-GLIF-iks) *noun* writing used by ancient Egyptians, made up of pictures and symbols

infantry (IN-fuhn-tree) *noun* the part of an army that fights on foot

legislature (LEJ-iss-lay-chur) *noun* a group of people who have the power to make or change laws for a country or state

monarch (MON-ark) *noun* a ruler who inherits his or her position

Napoleonic Code (nuh-POLE-ee-on-ik CODE) *noun* the first modern organized body of law governing France, established by Napoleon in 1804

regiment (REJ-uh-muhnt) *noun* a military unit made up of two to four battalions

republic (ri-PUB-lik) *noun* a form of government in which citizens have the power to elect representatives who manage the government

revolution (rev-uh-LOO-shuhn) *noun* an uprising by the people of a country that changes the country's system of government

Royalist (ROI-uhl-ist) *noun* a person who supported the monarchy during the French Revolution

treason (TREE-zuhn) *noun* the crime of betraying one's country by spying for another country or helping an enemy during a war

tsar (ZAR) noun the emperor of Russia before the Russian Revolution of 1917

vanquish (VANG-kwish) verb to defeat or conquer an enemy in battle

vengeance (VEN-juhnss) noun punishment inflicted in retaliation for an injury or offense

FIND OUT MORE

Here are some books and websites with more information about Napoleon and his times.

BOOKS AND ARTICLES

Arnold, James R. The Aftermath of the French Revolution (Aftermath of History). Minneapolis: Twenty-First Century Books, 2009. (160 pages) *Read about the circumstances that led to Napoleon's seizure of power in France after the French Revolution.*

DiConsiglio, John. Robespierre: Master of the Guillotine. New York: Franklin Watts, 2008. (128 pages) *A gripping account of the French Revolution that set the stage for Napoleon's rise to power.*

Greenblatt, Miriam. Napoleon Bonaparte and Imperial France (Rulers and Their Times). New York: Marshall Cavendish Benchmark Books, 2006. (96 pages) *A vivid description of Napoleon's life and times.*

Nardo, Don. France (Enchantment of the World, Second Series). New York: Children's Press, 2007. (144 pages) *Describes the history, geography, and culture of France.*

Obstfeld, Raymond, ed. Napoleon Bonaparte (People Who Made History). San Diego: Greenhaven Press, 2001. (202 pages) *A series of essays exploring Napoleon's impact on the history of Europe and the world.*

Streissguth, Thomas. The Napoleonic Wars: Defeat of the Grand Army. San Diego: Lucent Books, 2003. (112 pages) *Discusses Napoleon's leadership during the Napoleonic Wars.*

WEBSITES

http://chnm.gmu.edu/revolution *This comprehensive site includes real letters and documents from the French Revolution, as well as images, maps, and even songs.*

http://www.napoleonicsociety.com/english/frameSetAccueil_Eng.htm *The website of the International Napoleonic Society, an organization devoted to the study of the Napoleonic Era.*

http://www.napoleon.org/en/kids/index.asp *The educational page of the Fondation Napoleon, an organization committed to the study of Napoleon and his times.*

http://www.pbs.org/empires/napoleon *This online companion to the PBS special* Napoleon *includes a timeline, mini-biographies, and an interactive simulator of the Battle of Waterloo.*

AUTHOR'S NOTE AND BIBLIOGRAPHY

I didn't know that there was such a thing as history until one day in third grade when my regular teacher got her car stuck in the snow and was late to school. We had a student teacher assigned to our classroom who did something extraordinary. She pulled down a map that had been there the whole time, showed us France and Europe, and began to talk about a man named Napoleon. She even buttoned up her cardigan to show us the way he liked to rest his hand inside his waistcoat in the days before clothes had pockets.

I was spellbound. Was this even legal? To be at school learning about true and interesting stories instead of laboring over long division or spelling?

I'm sure Napoleon would have been pleased and not a bit surprised to discover that, for one student at least, all of history began with him.

The following sources have been the most useful in writing this book:

Burleigh, Nina. **Mirage: Napoleon's Scientists and the Unveiling of Egypt**. New York: Harper, 2007.

Cronin, Vincent. **Napoleon**. New York: HarperCollins, 1994.

Herold, J. Christopher. **The Age of Napoleon**. New York: Houghton Mifflin, 2002.

Horne, Alistair. **The Age of Napoleon**. New York: Modern Library, 2006.

Johnson, Paul. **Napoleon**. New York: Viking Penguin, 2002.

McLynn, Frank. **Napoleon: A Biography**. New York: Arcade, 2002.

Schom, Alan. **Napoleon Bonaparte**. New York: HarperCollins, 1997.

Smith, William H. C. **The Bonapartes: The History of a Dynasty**. New York: Hambledon and London, 2005.

Strathern, Paul. **Napoleon in Egypt**. New York: Bantam, 2007.

Willms, Johannes. **Napoleon and St. Helena: On the Island of Exile**. London: F Publishing, 2007.

—Kimberley Heuston